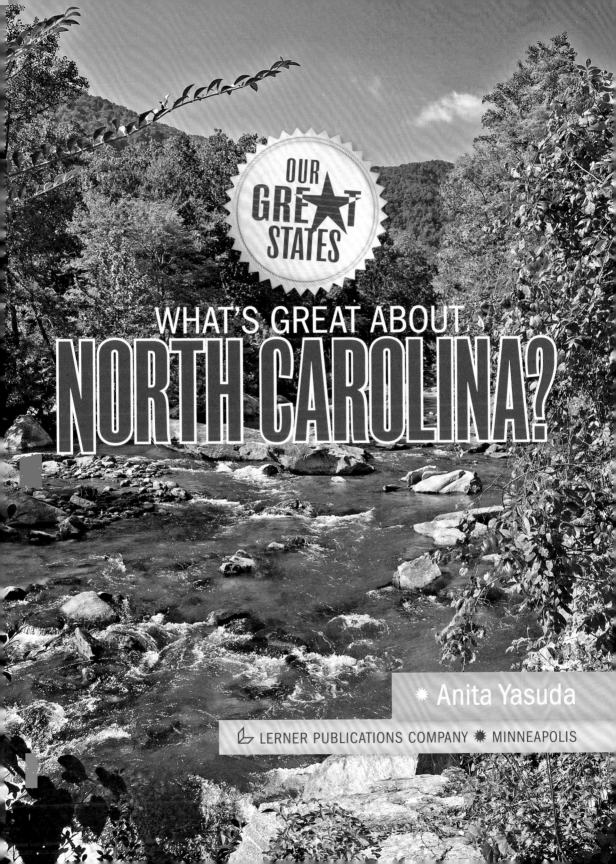

OUR GREAT STATES

WHAT'S GREAT ABOUT
NORTH CAROLINA?

✴ Anita Yasuda

LERNER PUBLICATIONS COMPANY ✴ MINNEAPOLIS

CONTENTS

NORTH CAROLINA
WELCOMES YOU! ✳ 4

Content Consultant: Mark Thompson,
Department of History, University of North
Carolina at Pembroke

Lerner Publications Company
A division of Lerner Publishing Group, Inc.
241 First Avenue North
Minneapolis, MN 55401 USA

For reading levels and more information, look
up this title at www.lernerbooks.com.

Main body text set in ITC Franklin Gothic Std
Book Condensed 12/15.
Typeface provided by Adobe Systems.

Library of Congress Cataloging-in-Publication
Data

Yasuda, Anita.
    What's great about North Carolina? / by
Anita Yasuda.
        pages   cm. — (Our great states)
    Includes index.
      ISBN 978-1-4677-3339-7 (lib. bdg. :
alk. paper)
      ISBN 978-1-4677-4715-8 (eBook)
    1. North Carolina—Juvenile literature.
2. North Carolina—Guidebooks—Juvenile
literature. I. Title.
F254.3.Y37 2015
975.6—dc23   2014002557

Manufactured in the United States of America
1 - PC – 7/15/14

NORTH CAROLINA Welcomes You!

Greetings from the Tar Heel State! This is a place like no other. It has pine-covered mountains. It has swamps filled with mossy trees. You'll also find miles of beautiful, sandy beaches. There's a lot to see and do in North Carolina. Read on to learn about ten great places to visit. Get ready to find out what makes North Carolina great!

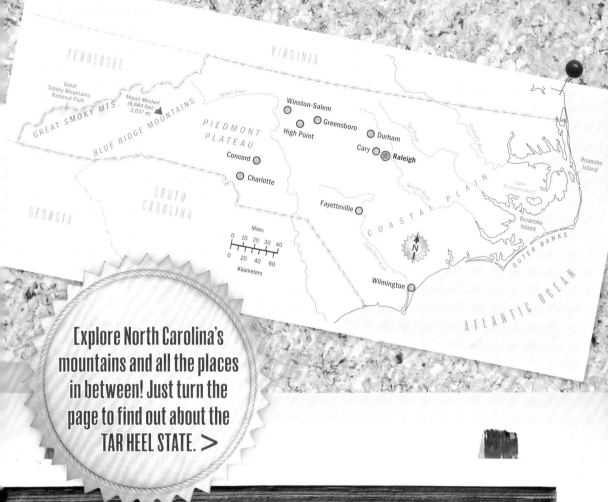

Explore North Carolina's mountains and all the places in between! Just turn the page to find out about the TAR HEEL STATE. >

OCRACOKE ISLAND

> Take a trip into North Carolina's pirate past at Ocracoke Island. This was a popular hangout for pirates in the 1700s.

One famous pirate called himself Edward Teach. But you may know him by the name Blackbeard. This fearsome outlaw had a hideout on Ocracoke Island. Blackbeard was killed in a battle that took place just offshore. British naval officers cut off the pirate's head! You can still visit the channel where Blackbeard's ship, *Queen Anne's Revenge*, sank. It's known as Teach's Hole, after the pirate.

Later, join in a ghost walk. Guides tell spooky stories about the island's history. Legend says Blackbeard's ghost is still looking for his head!

Have you ever dreamed of becoming a pirate for the day? Then hop aboard the *Sea Gypsy*. The ship's crew will take you on a pirate adventure. You will dress up in pirate costumes, play pirate games, and fire water cannons. You can even hunt for treasure. You won't have to walk the plank. But you *will* walk away with great stories!

Ocracoke Lighthouse was built in 1823 to help guide sailors through the dangerous waters surrounding Ocracoke Island.

Pirate Edward Teach spent time on Ocracoke in the 1700s. Some say his ghost still haunts the island.

RALEIGH

> Raleigh is a city that can't be missed. North Carolina's capital has been an important city for hundreds of years. But it's not just about visiting old sites. Raleigh's downtown is buzzing with activity.

The city's super-cool museums are the highlight of Raleigh. The Marbles Kids Museum is full of hands-on fun. Kids rule at the Around Town exhibit. Pretend you are a firefighter, a farmer, or a veterinarian. Then head over to the IdeaWorks gallery. This fun exhibit lets kids build what they imagine. You can design a race car. Or you can build a skyscraper out of blocks.

The North Carolina Museum of Natural Sciences is another fun museum in Raleigh. This is the oldest museum in North Carolina. It is also the biggest natural history museum in the Southeast. You'll learn everything you ever wanted to know about science and nature. Come here in September for BugFest. This yearly celebration is all about everything creepy and crawly. Get your face painted or play bug bingo. Brave visitors can even try tasty snacks made of bugs!

WALTER RALEIGH

SIR WALTER RALEIGH

The city of Raleigh was named for Sir Walter Raleigh. In the 1580s, England's Queen Elizabeth I sent him to claim land in North America. Raleigh tried twice to set up colonies in what is now North Carolina. Both attempts failed. The area wasn't settled until the 1600s. That's when settlers from Virginia, who were looking for farmland, came to the area.

Visitors can get an up-close look at an ancient shark jaw at the North Carolina Museum of Natural Sciences.

OCONALUFTEE INDIAN VILLAGE

> The Oconaluftee Indian Village is a special place. Nestled in the woods, it is a model of a Cherokee village from the 1760s. But it is more than a group of buildings. At the village, you will discover the stories and the history of the Cherokee.

Set out on your own or with a guide to experience Cherokee life. You will feel like a time traveler. Reenactors make canoes from logs. People weave with bright threads. The village also has arrowhead-making and mask-carving demonstrations.

You might hear a traditional Cherokee story or see a play. Do you love music? Then join in the Friendship Dance. Soon you will be stomping your feet in time with the drums. You may even learn a few words of Cherokee by the end of the day!

THE CHEROKEE

The Cherokee have lived in North Carolina's Appalachian Mountains for thousands of years. But Europeans spread out across the Southeast from the 1600s to the 1800s. The settlers wanted more land. In the 1830s, the US government forced the Cherokee to leave North Carolina. They moved to present-day Oklahoma. Their forced journey became known as the Trail of Tears. Thousands died along the way.

Workers create dugout canoes from giant logs, the same way the Cherokee did in the 1700s.

TWEETSIE RAILROAD

> *Tweeeeeeeeeeeet!* Can you hear the whistle of North Carolina's famous steam-powered train? It is chugging through the Blue Ridge Mountains. The train is the main attraction at North Carolina's first theme park.

The railroad began in 1882. The train once traveled through Tennessee. From there, it went to North Carolina. Local people nicknamed it Tweetsie. That's what the train's whistle sounded like to them.

Visitors to the park love the 3-mile (5-kilometer) ride on the train. But they had better look out for train robbers! Actors playing robbers, cowboys, or American Indians might board the train. Passengers never know what they will experience!

Back in the park's town, you can explore an old general store, a blacksmith's shop, and a jail. A chairlift takes visitors up to a gold mine. Everyone has fun panning for gold and gems!

After your mining expedition, check out the amusement park's zoo. It is complete with ninety animals, including miniature horses. Then enjoy the park's rides and fair games. Maybe you will win a prize!

In the past, the Tweetsie Railroad carried lumber and passengers.

The Tweetsie Railroad runs through the stunning scenery of the Blue Ridge Mountains.

GREAT SMOKY MOUNTAINS NATIONAL PARK

> Great Smoky Mountains National Park is one of the largest US national parks. It was created in 1934. Nine million visitors come to see its stunning scenery each year.

Start your visit with a hike back in time at the Mountain Farm Museum. This gives you the chance to see what a real farm community looked like one hundred years ago. It has a waterwheel-powered mill and historic log cabins. Can you imagine what life may have been like in these mountains? Tend the fire at the blacksmith's shop. You can even make a dinner bell to take home.

Afterward, explore the miles of trails. You can travel on foot or on horseback. The trails will take you past beautiful waterfalls. Keep your eyes peeled for wildlife. You may see deer, wild turkeys, or bears!

Come during the late spring to see the park's special visitors. Each night in early June, thousands of fireflies flash across the hills. It's an amazing show.

You may see horses grazing among the log cabins at the Mountain Farm Museum.

NORTH CAROLINA TAR

Pine trees cover much of North Carolina. These were once a very important part of the state's economy. The trees produce tar. In the 1700s and the 1800s, this tar was sold throughout North America and England. It was used for shipbuilding. The tar was very sticky. It sometimes got stuck on people's feet. Some people think this is why North Carolina's nickname is the Tar Heel State.

WRIGHT BROTHERS NATIONAL MONUMENT

> Once upon a time, people dreamed of flying like the birds. They built fantastic machines. None worked very well. Then two brothers from Ohio came along. Their names were Wilbur and Orville Wright.

In 1900, the brothers began testing gliders at Kill Devil Hills in North Carolina. They chose the site because of its tall dunes. The sand provided a soft landing. The site also had a steady wind. In 1903, the Wright brothers used Kill Devil Hills to test an airplane they had built. On December 17, 1903, the brothers flew the first powered airplane.

This area is now a 400-acre (162-hectare) park. Race a friend up Big Kill Devil Hill. The Wright brothers took off from this sand dune. Check out the 60-foot-tall (18-meter) memorial to the Wright brothers. Can you spot the white boulders? They mark the spot where the brothers' crafts took off.

The visitors center displays models of the Wright brothers' 1902 glider and 1903 plane. While here, learn how to build a kite. Then fly your kite on the Wright airfield where the brothers flew their aircraft. Up, up, and away!

The Wright brothers built and tested planes throughout the early 1900s.

WILBUR
WRIGHT
ORVILLE
WRIGHT

ON OF THE CONQUEST OF THE AIR

END OF 1st FLIGHT
TIME: 12 SECONDS
DISTANCE: 120 FT.
DEC. 17, 1903
PILOT: ORVILLE

Read the white boulders to find out more information about the Wright brothers' flights.

WILBUR

CAPE HATTERAS NATIONAL SEASHORE

> Cape Hatteras National Seashore is a great place for a day at the beach. It is known for its miles of beaches piled high with shells.

Cape Hatteras has so many fun things to do. You'll find sand dunes to run up and clams to uncover. Hop in a kayak to explore the seashore by water. Back on land, you can look for birds or hunt for seashells. At dusk, you may see ghost crabs scuttling across the beaches. They are named for their ghostly white appearance.

In the 1700s, Cape Hatteras became known as Graveyard of the Atlantic. The ocean here is full of sandbars. Many ships sank after hitting these sandbars. Lighthouses were built to warn ships of the danger. Cape Hatteras Lighthouse looks like a giant stick of candy with black-and-white stripes. At 198 feet (60 m), it is the tallest brick lighthouse in the United States. Get ready to climb. It will take 269 steps to get you to the top. The view is worth the climb!

THE ROANOKE MYSTERY

In 1587, English settlers started a colony on Roanoke Island, near Cape Hatteras. But soon, the settlers ran short of supplies. The governor returned to England. He came back three years later. The settlers were gone. But he found the word *Croatoan* carved into a tree. Historians still don't know what happened to the Roanoke settlers. At the time, Hatteras Island was known as Croatoan Island. Some think the settlers may have moved there.

Pelicans are one of many birds you can look for at Cape Hatteras.

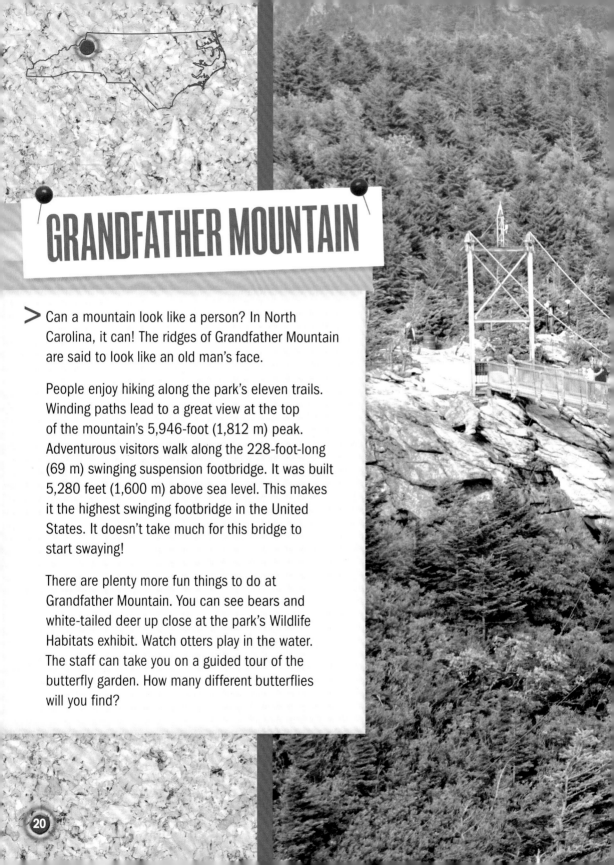

GRANDFATHER MOUNTAIN

> Can a mountain look like a person? In North Carolina, it can! The ridges of Grandfather Mountain are said to look like an old man's face.

People enjoy hiking along the park's eleven trails. Winding paths lead to a great view at the top of the mountain's 5,946-foot (1,812 m) peak. Adventurous visitors walk along the 228-foot-long (69 m) swinging suspension footbridge. It was built 5,280 feet (1,600 m) above sea level. This makes it the highest swinging footbridge in the United States. It doesn't take much for this bridge to start swaying!

There are plenty more fun things to do at Grandfather Mountain. You can see bears and white-tailed deer up close at the park's Wildlife Habitats exhibit. Watch otters play in the water. The staff can take you on a guided tour of the butterfly garden. How many different butterflies will you find?

Otters are just one of the many animals you may see while hiking near Grandfather Mountain.

Can you find the outline of an old man's face in Grandfather Mountain?

23

BILTMORE ESTATE

> Believe it or not, North Carolina is home to a huge French chateau, or castle. It is called the Biltmore Estate. Millionaire George Vanderbilt fell in love with the hills of Asheville in 1888. He wanted to build himself something special and beautiful there. He decided to build Biltmore Estate. Construction ended in 1895.

Biltmore is the United States' largest home. The building stretches more than 4 acres (1.6 ha). You can go on a tour of the home. It has 250 rooms and 65 fireplaces. The home's library has ten thousand books. Biltmore also has an indoor pool and a bowling alley. Try to imagine what it might be like to live there!

Make sure to head out to the grounds once you're done inside. You'll find plenty more to explore. Count the gargoyles on the roof. Take pictures with the stone lions that guard the entrance to the chateau. Then see if you can find your way out of the maze. Be sure to stomp on grapes at the winery. The French Broad River runs through the estate. This river runs for more than 200 miles (320 km) all the way into Tennessee. Visitors to Biltmore can take a fly-fishing class. Finish your visit by relaxing on the water. You can float through the estate on a river raft.

As you explore the grounds, look for gargoyles and other interesting statues.

Enjoy a ride in a wooden rowboat on the French Broad River.

23

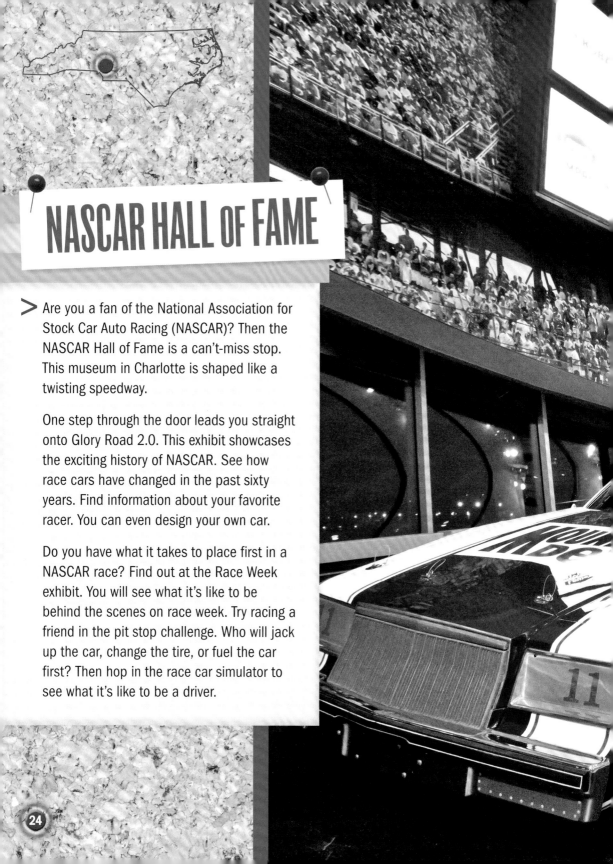

NASCAR HALL OF FAME

> Are you a fan of the National Association for Stock Car Auto Racing (NASCAR)? Then the NASCAR Hall of Fame is a can't-miss stop. This museum in Charlotte is shaped like a twisting speedway.

One step through the door leads you straight onto Glory Road 2.0. This exhibit showcases the exciting history of NASCAR. See how race cars have changed in the past sixty years. Find information about your favorite racer. You can even design your own car.

Do you have what it takes to place first in a NASCAR race? Find out at the Race Week exhibit. You will see what it's like to be behind the scenes on race week. Try racing a friend in the pit stop challenge. Who will jack up the car, change the tire, or fuel the car first? Then hop in the race car simulator to see what it's like to be a driver.

See how fast you can fill a race car tire with air at the Race Week exhibit.

The NASCAR Hall of Fame celebrates some of the best race car drivers in the world.

YOUR TOP TEN!

You've read about ten awesome things to see and do in North Carolina. Now think about what your North Carolina top ten list would include. If you were planning a North Carolina vacation, what would you like to see? Write down your top ten list. You can turn your list into a booklet. Just add drawings or pictures from the Internet or magazines.

NORTH CAROLINA BY MAP

> MAP KEY

- ⭐ Capital city
- ⚪ City
- ⚪ Point of interest
- 🔺 Highest elevation
- –·– State border

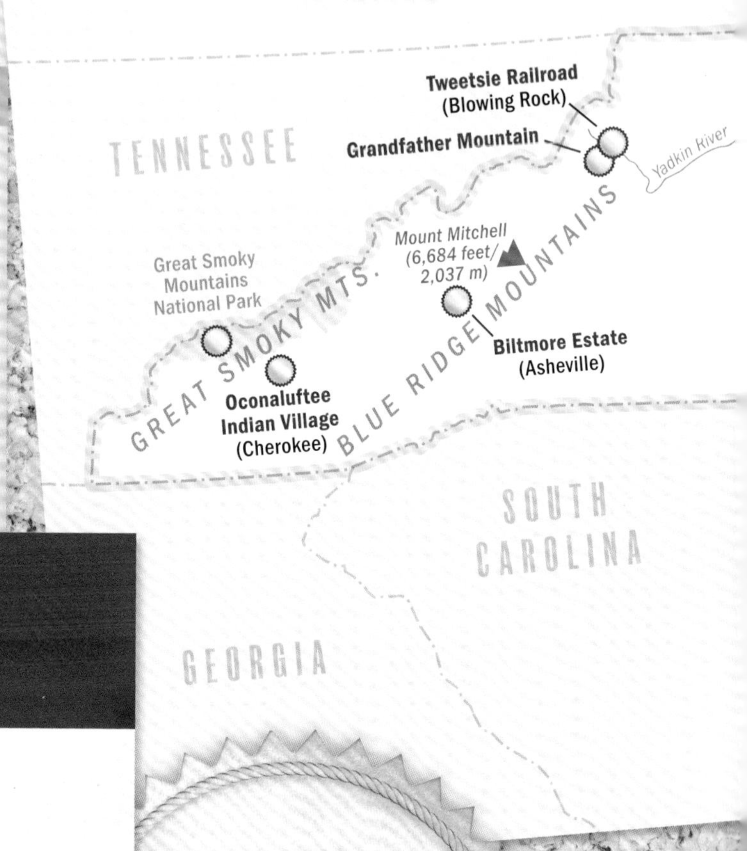

TENNESSEE

Tweetsie Railroad
(Blowing Rock)

Grandfather Mountain

Yadkin River

Great Smoky
Mountains
National Park

GREAT SMOKY MTS.

Mount Mitchell
(6,684 feet/
2,037 m)

BLUE RIDGE MOUNTAINS

Biltmore Estate
(Asheville)

**Oconaluftee
Indian Village**
(Cherokee)

**SOUTH
CAROLINA**

GEORGIA

MAY 20th 1775

N ⭐ C

APRIL 12th 1776

**Visit www.lerneresource.com to learn
more about the state flag of North Carolina.**

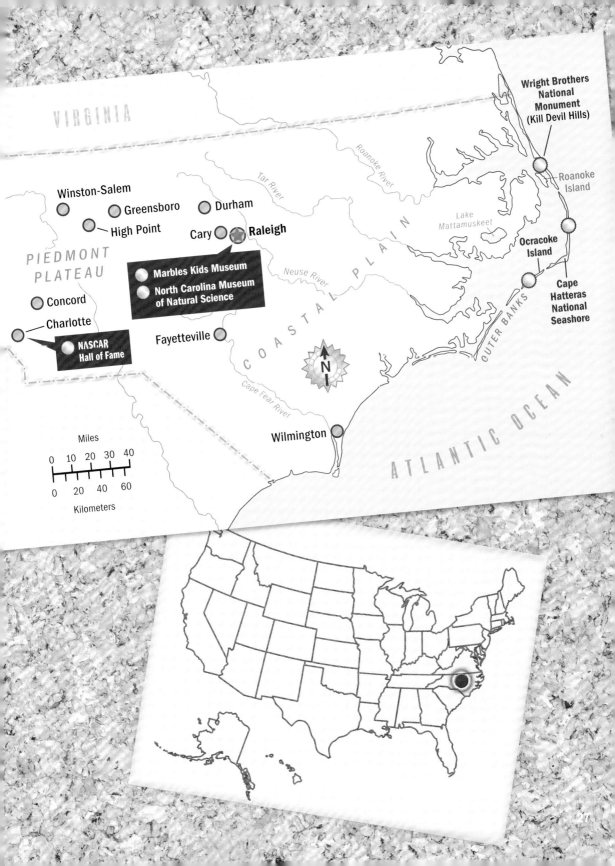

VIRGINIA

Roanoke River

Tar River

Lake Mattamuskeet

Wright Brothers National Monument (Kill Devil Hills)

Roanoke Island

Winston-Salem

Greensboro

Durham

High Point

Cary

Raleigh

PIEDMONT PLATEAU

Marbles Kids Museum

North Carolina Museum of Natural Science

Neuse River

Ocracoke Island

Cape Hatteras National Seashore

Concord

Charlotte

NASCAR Hall of Fame

Fayetteville

C O A S T A L   P L A I N

O U T E R   B A N K S

N

Cape Fear River

ATLANTIC OCEAN

Wilmington

Miles

0   10   20   30   40

0   20   40   60

Kilometers

NORTH CAROLINA FACTS

NICKNAME: The Tar Heel State

SONG: "The Old North State" by William Gaston

MOTTO: *Esse Quam Videri*, or "To Be, Rather Than to Seem"

> **FLOWER:** dogwood

TREE: longleaf pine

BIRD: cardinal

ANIMAL: gray squirrel

> **FOOD:** sweet potato

DATE AND RANK OF STATEHOOD: November 21, 1789; the 12th state

> **CAPITAL:** Raleigh

AREA: 52,663 square miles (136,397 sq. km)

AVERAGE JANUARY TEMPERATURE: 41°F (5°C)

AVERAGE JULY TEMPERATURE: 70°F (21°C)

POPULATION AND RANK: 9,752,073; 11th (2012)

MAJOR CITIES AND POPULATIONS: Charlotte (775,202), Raleigh (423,179), Greensboro (277,080), Durham (239,358); Winston-Salem (234,349)

NUMBER OF US CONGRESS MEMBERS: 13 representatives, 2 senators

NUMBER OF ELECTORAL VOTES: 15

NATURAL RESOURCES: clay, coal, crushed stone, feldspar, fish, flagstone, gemstones, granite, lumber, marble, seafood, water

> **AGRICULTURAL PRODUCTS:** barley, chicken, cotton, fruits, hay, tobacco

MANUFACTURED GOODS: cleaning products, computer and electronic products, cotton cloth, furniture, pharmaceutical products, tobacco products

STATE HOLIDAYS AND CELEBRATIONS: North Carolina State Fair, North Carolina Apple Festival, African American Cultural Festival

GLOSSARY

blacksmith: someone who makes and fixes objects by heating and shaping iron

cape: a piece of land that juts out into the sea

chateau: a French castle

colony: a territory ruled by a country far away

dune: a hill of sand that has been piled up by the wind

economy: the system in which goods are produced, bought, and sold in a place

exhibit: a display of something

gargoyle: a statue of a human or an animal used as a waterspout

glider: an aircraft that has no motor

memorial: a structure built to remind people of a person or event

reenactor: a person who acts out historical events

sandbar: a ridge of sand offshore

settler: a person who goes to a new land to live

simulator: a machine used to imitate how an object or action looks or feels

veterinarian: a doctor who treats animals

FURTHER INFORMATION

Cunningham, Kevin. *The North Carolina Colony.* New York: Children's Press, 2012. Explore the lives of colonialists in North Carolina with text and pictures.

Donaldson, Madeline. *Pirates, Scoundrels, and Scallywags.* Minneapolis: Lerner Publications, 2013. Learn more about the lives of the pirates, including the legendary Blackbeard.

Jerome, Kate Boehm. *North Carolina: What's So Great about This State?* Charleston, SC: Arcadia Publishing, 2011. This book is a fun introduction to North Carolina's history, geography, and people.

North Carolina Encyclopedia
http://ncpedia.org
This site highlights North Carolina's people and culture. There is information on natural resources, lots of wildlife images, and articles.

North Carolina Secretary of State Kids Page
http://www.secretary.state.nc.us/kidspg
Visit this official state site to learn more about North Carolina's history, state symbols, legends, and ghost stories.

Official Website of North Carolina
http://www.ncgov.com
Explore this site to discover North Carolina's history from American Indian archeological sites to Civil War trails and legislative tours.

INDEX

PHOTO ACKNOWLEDGMENTS

The images in this book are used with the permission of: © Harry B. Lamb/Shutterstock Images, p. 1; © Steve Bower/Shutterstock Images, p. 4; © Laura Westlund/Independent Picture Service, pp. 5 (top), 26–27; © Les Palenik /Thinkstock, p. 5 (bottom); © Jill Lang/Thinkstock, pp. 6–7; © Jorge Moro/Shutterstock Images, p. 7 (left); © Getty Images/Thinkstock, p. 7 (right); Library of Congress, pp. 8 (LC-DIG-highsm-02420), 10 (LC-USZ62-90958); © Spirit of America /Shutterstock Images, pp. 8–9; © Jeff Greenberg /Alamy, p. 9; © John Elk III/Alamy, pp. 10–11; © Eye Ubiquitous/Glow Images, p. 11; © Andre Jenny Stock Connection Worldwide/Newscom, pp. 12–13, 21 (bottom); © Dave Allen Photography/Shutterstock Images, pp. 13 (left), 14–15; © Ivan Dmitri/Michael Ochs Archives/Getty Images, p. 13 (right); © Glow Images, p. 15 (top); © BSPollard/iStockphoto, p. 15 (bottom); © sgoodwin4813/iStockphoto, pp. 16–17; © Photos.com/Thinkstock, p. 17 (top); © Marc Norman/iStockphoto, p. 17 (bottom); © Jill Lang /iStockphoto, pp. 18–19; © North Wind/North Wind Picture Archives, p. 19 (top); © Sherry Yates Young/Shutterstock Images, p. 19 (bottom); © sshepard/iStockphoto, pp. 20–21; © marshall9093/iStockphoto, p. 21 (top); © Fotoluminate LLC/Shutterstock Images, pp. 22–23; © Thom Morris/iStockphoto, p. 23 (top); © iStockphoto/Thinkstock, p. 23 (bottom); © Leon T. Switzer/Icon SMI, pp. 24–25; © Chris Keane/Icon SMI, p. 25 (left); © Denton Rumsey /Shutterstock Images, p. 25 (right); © nicoolay /iStockphoto, p. 26; © Jorge Antonio/iStockphoto, p. 29 (top); © adlifemarketing/iStockphoto, p. 29 (middle top); © Legacy Images/Shutterstock Images, p. 29 (middle bottom); © fotolinchen /iStockphoto, p. 29 (bottom).

Cover: © iStockphoto.com/WerksMedia (mountains); Mark Turner/Wikimedia Commons (Raleigh); © Jared C. Tilton/Getty Images for NASCAR; © Walter Arce/Dreamstime.com (Wright Brothers Memorial); © Laura Westlund/ Independent Picture Service (map); © iStockphoto. com/fpm (seal); © iStockphoto.com/vicm (pushpins); © iStockphoto.com /benz190 (corkboard).